Bugs, Slugs
& Other Invaders

hamlyn

50 ways to beat
garden enemies

Bugs, Slugs
& Other Invaders

Sarah Ford

In memory of May

An Hachette Livre UK Company
www.hachettelivre.co.uk
First published in Great Britain in 2006 by Hamlyn, a division of
Octopus Publishing Group Ltd, 2–4 Heron Quays, London E14 4JP
www.octopusbooks.co.uk
Copyright © Octopus Publishing Group Ltd 2006

Distributed in the United States and Canada by
Sterling Publishing Co., Inc., 387 Park Avenue South,
New York, NY 10016–8810

ISBN: 978-0-600-61520-0

A CIP catalogue record for this book is available from the
British Library

Printed and bound in China

10 9 8 7 6 5 4 3

Notes

While all reasonable care has been taken during the preparation of this
book, neither the publisher nor the editors nor the author can accept
responsibility for any consequences arising from the use of this
information (especially if dining on garden snails).

Always read the manufacturer's instructions carefully before using any
chemical or organic pesticides. Keep them away from animals and
children, but wield gleefully in front of your garden enemies.

Contents

The bug stops here!

Even professional gardeners will tell you that they have had some spectacular gardening failures. Nature is downright unpredictable: it always has been and always will be – that is why it's so exciting and challenging. However, waking to find your favourite plant razed to the ground can be more than a little disheartening. You may be tempted to throw in the trowel – not only do garden bugs come in all shapes and sizes, but there are armies of them just waiting to attack the minute you let down your guard. But don't be put off. With just a little knowledge and the occasional helping hand, you *can* stay in control and your garden *will* flourish!

Forewarned is forearmed

Find out what you're up against and the battle is almost won. Do your bugs eat the roots or the leaves, do they attack by day or under cover of night? What time of year do they bear offspring, what do they like and dislike? Gathering such information is invaluable when formulating your battle plan.

Friend or foe?

Not all bugs are enemies – there are a good number of garden heroes too and, if left to it, they will merrily do your job for you. Create the right environment for the good guys and they will return your garden to order. They will eat the baddies, improve the soil and pollinate your flowers. Using chemicals in the garden should always be a last resort. An insecticide will not discriminate between a garden friend and a garden enemy and can do more harm than good.

The good, the bad and the ugly

Good: Ladybugs, earthworms, centipedes, bees, toads, frogs, hedgehogs, butterflies, hoverflies, garden spiders, swallows and robins. Welcome these little fellows with open arms. They will restore balance in the garden and fight the bad guys, unwittingly protecting your plants. (See pages 70–91 to learn more.)

Bad: Red ants, earwigs, wasps and woodlice. While these creatures will not do any lasting damage to your garden, they don't bring any benefits either. Best to do away with them if you can.

Ugly: Aphids, caterpillars, scale insects, vine weevils, slugs and snails – the gardener's most wanted! These evil little critters are hated by all gardeners because they destroy everything in their path. No plant is safe with them around.

11

And so to battle

Now that you know what you're dealing with, battle can commence. While it could be said that Mother Nature has her own agenda, it's always good to give her a helping hand. One of the best things a conscientious gardener can do is spring-clean the garden. By clearing away all the debris you will also dispose of any bugs that have been hiding out during winter months, ready to re-emerge bigger and hungrier than ever when the weather warms up. Rake up any mulch from flower and vegetable beds (this can go into the compost bin for reuse). Feed the plants and apply compost. Turn over the soil and pay close attention to any unwelcome eggs that may be about to hatch . . .

Back down to earth

The joy of having a garden is partly about watching nature do its own thing. Inevitably, you will win some battles and lose others. Even with your best endeavours, some plants will fall prey to your garden enemies. Try to remain philosophical, enjoy your successes and don't get too hung up on the failures. Show a little bug love – after all, you can't control nature and that's a good thing.

Flying foe

The cold shower

Aphids are one of the most common garden pests. They show no mercy and will attack a plant in its entirety.

1. Unleash a strong jet of cold water from your garden hose.

2. Several blasts should dislodge all aphids and send them clean to their graves!

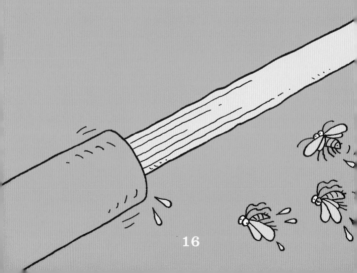

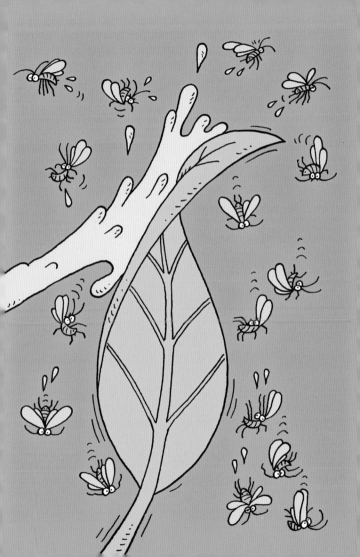

Poached eggs please

You can significantly reduce the survival rate of aphids by planting the right flowers and making your garden a hotspot for aphid predators.

1. Grow plants that lure beneficial bugs to your garden. Poached egg plant, convolvulus and aster are ideal. These attract ladybugs, lacewings and hoverflies, all of whom simply love an aphid feast.

2. Let nature take its course and without fail the good guys will go to work on the bad guys.

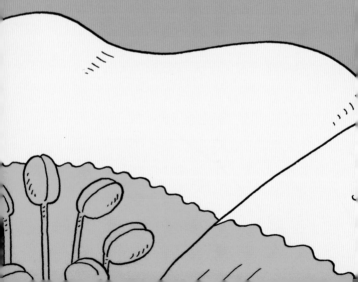

Bats in the belfry

Bats love eating aphids and are active in the early evening, when these small flying insects are found in abundance. To encourage bats you have to create the right environment.

1. Plant a border full of evening-scented plants, such as tobacco plant, honeysuckle, stocks and jasmine.

2. Not only will your garden smell delicious, but the bats will come swooping in to rid you of your aphid population.

Bring in those boys in blue

**Make your garden a haven for blue tits, who just
happen to be rather partial to aphid eggs.**

1. Plant a nesting box and leave out seeds and nuts for
your heroes to feed on (but not too many – you want
them to have healthy appetites). And keep your
birdbath topped up.

2. What blue tit could resist such a luxury hotel? With
aphid caviar on the menu, they'll keep coming back
for more.

Creepy crawlies

Weevil knievel

Vine weevils are nasty little leaf-munchers. The best way to get rid of them is by making sure they can't get to the feast in the first place. Your secret weapon is water – they just hate it.

1. Keep your favourite plants in pots standing in a watering tray.

2. Keep the tray topped up with water and your aquaphobic pests will be forced to stay away.

Disco dancing

Adult vine weevils come alive at dusk. Send these
slow-moving creatures an invite to the ugly bug ball
and you're guaranteed to score!

1. Wait for dusk to fall then stand at the ready,
flashlight in hand.

2. Seek out the enemy and pounce.

3. Dispose of your bounty as you see fit.

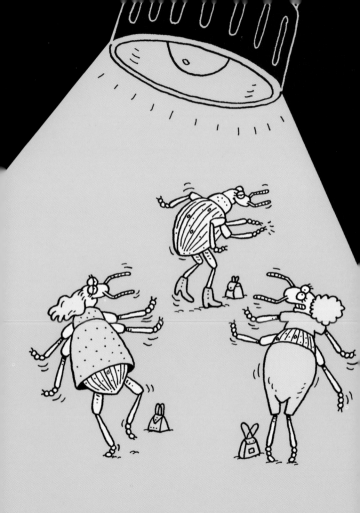

A meths a day . . .

Mealy bugs are soft, wingless insects that look a bit like clusters of white fluff and are found on the underside of leaves. They love plant sap and their sucking weakens their victims.

1. Dip an old toothbrush into methylated spirit and brush mealy bugs off any infected plant.

2. The meths will penetrate their outer coat and kill them almost immediately.

Shaken AND stirred

Earwigs love eating flowers, buds and leaves –
especially from chrysanthemums, dahlias and
clematis. Strike by day while they're sound asleep.

1. Give your flowers a good shake to dislodge any
sleeping earwigs.

2. If you're quick, they'll hit the floor still snoozing
and you can stamp on them before they know
anything about it.

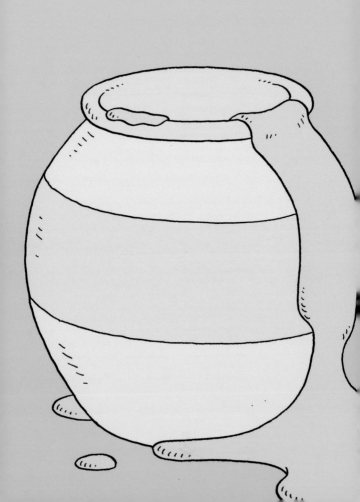

The honey trap

The earwig has a sweet tooth and can't resist peanut butter and honey. Here's how to set the perfect trap.

1. Add a little peanut butter and honey to some straw in a propped-up flowerpot.

2. Earwigs can't resist a quick snack and will head straight for the bounty.

3. At the end of the day, remove the straw and burn it before the little critters wake up.

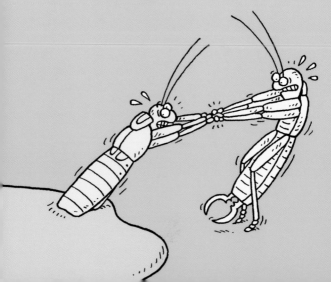

Time to get dead drunk

To wash down that peanut butter and honey
sandwich, earwigs like nothing more than a slurp
of beer. This can be their downfall.

1. Bury some beer cans in your garden with a little bit
of beer left in the bottom.

2. Earwigs will be lured to the bar by the thought of a
quick drink after work.

3. Once in they'll drown and can be disposed of the
following day.

Don't cross the line!

Ants do not like chalk. By drawing a simple chalk line you can create an insurmountable barrier between them and your plants.

1. Buy a box of classroom chalk.

2. Draw a chalk circle around your plants.

3. Watch in amazement as a troop of ants marches up to the line and stops abruptly, tripping over each other in the confusion. Your plants will be safe and sound on the other side.

Spice up shower time

Exploit the aversion of ants to the smell of cinnamon and cloves.

1. First locate the ants' nest.

2. Add a small bottle of cinnamon or clove oil to a full watering can.

3. Give the ants a spicy shower, sprinkling the contents of your can over their nest.

Suck 'em up

A simple, but effective, method for getting rid of an entire ants' nest.

1. Watch the movements of your ants in order to locate their nest.

2. Get out your vacuum cleaner and suck 'em all up. Job done!

Get the kids on the case

Caterpillars are usually attracted to certain sorts of plant, for example the cabbage white likes eating cabbages and radishes. Enlist the services of your children to collect the caterpillars for you. They will be thrilled and the task could keep them occupied for the whole afternoon!

1. Invest in a couple of bars of chocolate in case enthusiasm starts to dwindle early on and offer a prize for the biggest caterpillar.

2. Re-house your caterpillars in the compost bin where there is plenty of rotting vegetation to keep them happy.

Dig the leather jacket

Leather jackets are the larvae of the crane fly, or daddy-longlegs. They burrow under grass, feeding on the roots and causing the grass to yellow. They are also rather partial to your greens, strawberries and potatoes.

1. Gently turn over your soil during summer months to expose the larvae.

2. Wait for the birds to swoop in and snap up these tasty morsels. Starlings are particularly fond of leather jackets and gather in groups in infested areas.

Furry invaders

My cat's bigger than your cat

Fed up with the neighbour's cat using your border as a litter tray? Then it's time for a trip to the zoo for some lion dung – that'll keep kitty away.

1. Armed with a plastic bag and a shovel, befriend a lion keeper and ask him to scoop some poop.

2. An easier option? Buy some lion dung from a garden centre. Spread your garden liberally with the pellets and watch Tiddles turn tail in disgust.

41

Water pistols at dawn

This does involve you lying in wait for kitty, but
nothing beats the satisfaction of a direct hit.

1. Buy the biggest and best water pistol you can find.

2. Take up your hiding place. Get ready, aim and fire!
A couple of good hits and you can be sure that puss
will be toileting elsewhere in future.

Pepper with that?

If lion dung is not for you, try the next best thing –
pepper. It's guaranteed to get up the nose of any
unsuspecting feline.

1. Grind lashings of pepper over your border or
wherever the offending cat has chosen as its toilet.

2. Stand back and watch puss give your garden a
wide berth.

If you can't beat 'em, join 'em

If all else fails you can always get a cat of your own
or, better still, a big dog.

1. Cats are notoriously territorial and will soon see off
any unwelcome guests entering the garden. You might
even find you become quite fond of your new furry
friend. And if you choose a ginger tom of the street-
fighter variety not only will it chase off the enemy, it
will repay your neighbours by using their garden as a
toilet and not yours.

2. If a cat is not for you, then surely a dog would do.
Not only is it man's best friend, but it will also take
endless pleasure in terrorizing neighbourhood cats.

Give the dog a bone

Dogs might keep the cats away, but they'll also dig up your back garden. Worse still, their toilet habits will turn your grass brown. Show a dog who's boss.

1. Dogs are a bit like children: they need to be entertained and taught boundaries in order to keep them out of trouble.

2. By providing a dog with its own toys for the garden you should avoid it chewing or digging up your precious plants.

A short sharp shock

**Mice will devour not only bulbs but also any peas
and beans in your treasured vegetable patch.**

1. Keep mice out by putting down a thick layer of
holly leaves wherever you've planted bulbs and seeds.

2. A few prickles in the bottom will make any bounty
suddenly less desirable and your mice will go off in
search of pastures new.

3. Holly leaves will also keep away furry felines in
search of a prime site for their toilet.

Tough plants fight back

Rabbits can make light work of the average garden, quickly destroying everything in their path. However, there are some plants that are just too tough for your average bunny.

1. Choose from a selection of plants with robust, leathery leaves: mahonia, elaeagnus, aucuba, osmanthus, acanthus, eryngium and phormium are all good options.

2. Plants with silvery foliage, such as lavender and artemisia, or with a lemon scent, are also less vulnerable to rabbit attack.

Bag a bunny

If rabbits are destroying your garden, it's time to take action. This will keep you fit, if nothing else.

1. Invest in a big fishing net, make a spyhole in your shed and camp out there.

2. When you see a bunny jump out, brandish your net and attempt to catch it.

3. If you're lucky, drive bunny out of town and release it. Threaten to turn it into rabbit stew if it ever comes back.

Flush 'em out

Waking to find your lawn covered in molehills is a far from happy experience. Moles are notoriously difficult to get rid of without calling in the professionals.

1. The best course of action is to persuade your moles to move house.

2. Pour one part cleaning fluid to twenty parts water into a watering can and flush the moles out of their holes. They have a strong sense of smell and this will be just a bit too much for them to deal with.

A foxy scent

Squirrels will eat your bulbs, nibble your buds and steal your birds' nuts. Call their bluff by fooling them that their arch enemy, the fox, is in the vicinity.

1. Visit your local garden centre and buy some fox urine powder.

2. Attach pouches of the powder to your bird table and shake the powder around your plants to simulate the presence of a fox. It will not be long before the squirrels take themselves off in search of a more fragrant home.

Lock up your plants

Probably one of the most successful ways of dealing with squirrels is to build a barrier around your plants.

1. Once you have finished planting bulbs in containers or a flowerbed, place some wire mesh over the top of the soil. To allow the plants to grow through, the mesh holes should have a diameter of about 6 cm (2½ in).

2. Remove the mesh for the spring months and watch your bulbs as they flourish.

Mark your territory

Deer do not like the smell of humans, so a good way
to deter them is to mark your territory in a very
distinctive way.

1. Encourage a male member of your family to pee
in the garden.

2. Make sure that he doesn't frighten any unsuspecting
neighbours. (Perhaps it would be better to collect the
urine in a bucket and distribute it.)

3. Wash your hands.

Soft and fragrant

Deer are put off by the smell of strong chemicals.

1. Buy a packet of fabric softener sheets from your local store.

2. Hang these about your garden, particularly on those plants and flowers that are targeted by deer.

Slimy, slithery
and scaly

Give them a buzz

Recent research has shown that caffeine has the power to stop slugs in their tracks! However, it's not known whether caffeine can also harm other garden dwellers and it's not yet fully licensed as a slug killer.

1. Fill a shallow container with some coffee or cola and place on the edge of your border, close to your prize plants.

2. Watch the slugs take that cola break, never to return!

Let them eat cat food

Slugs love cat and dog food, and a ready supply will coax them away from your plants. The food will also attract hedgehogs, who eat slugs – a double whammy! On the downside, it could have the adverse effect of encouraging visits from all the local cats and dogs – turning your garden into a giant pet toilet.

1. Bury some nearly empty cans of cat or dog food around slug-infested areas of your garden.

2. Temptation should be too great and, hopefully, slugs will fall in trying to get to the feast.

3. Pick out and destroy, or otherwise dispose of, the victims.

Dare them into the chicken run

Chickens are a great investment if your garden is big and rural: not only will chickens rid your garden of gastropods, they'll also ensure that you have a regular supply of eggs!

1. Choose three hens and one cock (so that your egg supply is guaranteed). Rhode Island Reds have insatiable appetites for slugs.

2. Set up a heavenly chicken coop at the bottom of your garden.

3. Let the chickens loose to do their thing and munch on all those juicy slugs – they will need little encouragement.

4. Enjoy eating eggs for breakfast in the knowledge that your garden is a slug-free zone and your plants are still beautiful.

Pass the salt

Salt is a highly effective slug killer, and one particularly favoured by young boys. It can have some negative consequences for your garden, however, so use it sparingly.

1. Under cover of the night, arm yourself with a flashlight and a handy pack of table salt.

2. Sprinkle each offending mollusc with just a few grains of salt.

3. Watch joyfully as it curls itself into a little ball; it'll be dead in seconds.

L'escargots et beurre aux herbes

Snails are simply delicious cooked with butter, garlic and herbs – you should try them.

1. Collect snails in a bucket by the dead of night.

2. Transfer them to an ovenproof dish and cover with a mixture of butter, garlic and herbs.

3. Cook in a hot oven and serve steaming hot.

It's in the bag

The best way to protect your plants is to tempt snails away with a tasty little snack.

1. Place a bag between your tender plants and fill it with all the things snails love, such as rotting lettuce, cat food and bran.

2. By morning the bag will be full of slugs and snails and can be disposed of as you see fit.

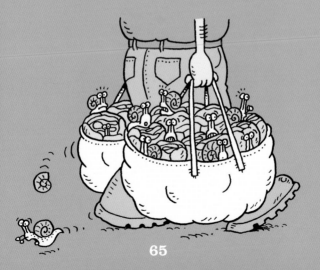

Treading the boards

Snails are always looking for somewhere to shelter;
they need to take rest in order to do maximum
damage to your plants.

1. If you have a vegetable garden, lay some planks or
boards between the beds.

2. Sneaky snails will soon search them out and hide in
clusters beneath them.

3. Turn the planks over and flick your slimy foe off
and into the compost bin.

Scratch their backs

Scale insects are tiny, limpet-like creatures that can be found stuck to the underside of leaves and on stems. They hide beneath a protective shell as they suck plant sap, weakening the plant. They can be a serious problem for shrubs and trees and are very difficult to get rid of.

1. The most effective way to dispose of these little critters is to scratch them off your plants, using your fingernails.

A dose of fatty acids

Use plant oils as an organic spray to combat scale insects and their offspring.

1. Spray vigilantly during the scale's hatching period.

2. You will have to be persistent in your applications, as scale insects are notoriously resistant.

The good guys

Ladies who lunch

Ladybugs can munch their way through up to forty aphids in one day and are great allies of the gardener. Plant their favourite flowers and let them lunch out daily with friends.

1. To encourage ladybugs into your garden, plant a selection of angelica, tansy and scented pelargoniums.

2. Ladybugs won't be able to resist such a gastronomic paradise and will soon settle down and have families. Your plants will then be aphid free.

Way to go worms

Worms are cool! They improve soil quality just by living, breathing and tunnelling through the stuff.

1. To make great compost, throw in a handful of worms and give a quick stir. Leave your wriggly pals to munch until your compost is the perfect consistency.

2. Now dig some manure into your soil. Good soil creates the right environment for happy worms who will breed and make even better soil. A worm's offspring can live for up to 12 years so try not to chop them up with your spade when you're digging.

Little lions from the internet

A quick and easy solution to the problem of garden pests is to ship in the lacewing babies, known as aphid lions.

1. Do some research on the internet – most good gardening websites will supply lacewing larvae. You can purchase about two hundred at a time.

2. Follow the instructions on the packet and let the little lions free to do their thing.

A boudoir for the ladies in lace

Lacewings are not predatory, but their babies
have voracious appetites and will eat anything that
moves. Make a home for the mums and they will
settle and breed.

1. Cut the bottom off a large, empty fizzy-drink
bottle. Place sticky-tape around the rough edge
at the bottom.

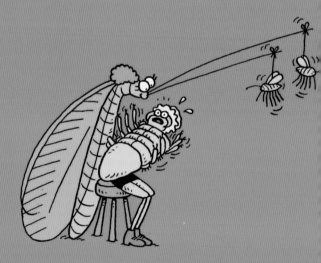

2. Cut some corrugated cardboard to the same length as the bottle. Roll it up and insert into the bottle so that it fits neatly.

3. Attach an elastic band and some string to the neck of the bottle and hang it near a window in autumn months. Move it into a shed for winter hibernation, then bring out again in spring.

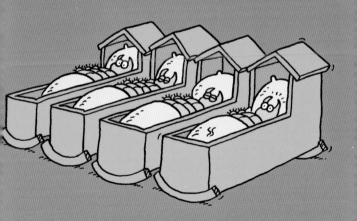

Build a hedgehog hideout

Hedgehogs need somewhere to hibernate. Prepare your garden for winter with their needs in mind.

1. Pile up twigs and logs at the bottom of the garden, or build a compost heap. Hedgehogs will be in seventh heaven.

2. Always check for signs of a spiky resident before setting light to any bonfires.

Scrambled eggs for breakfast

Hedgehogs are a welcome addition to any garden.
They eat slugs, bugs and grubs.

1. Hedgehogs need a helping hand in winter months.
Traditionally they have been fed bread and milk, but
they are lactose intolerant so this is not a good mix.

2. They far prefer a plate of scrambled egg.

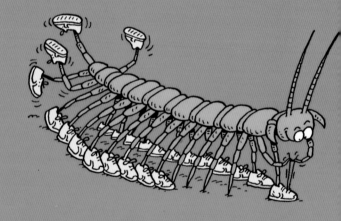

Give the centipede a hand tying its laces

A speedy centipede is quick to track down prey.

1. No slug or bad bug is safe with the centipede around. With thirty legs, this garden hero is practically impossible to get away from. Once it has got hold of a slug it will paralyse it with its venomous claws.

Impress the birds

During winter the best way to encourage birds into your garden is by feeding them delicacies like fat balls. Then, when it warms up, there will be plenty of feathered friends to feast on your uninvited bugs.

1. Heat some lard in a pan, add wild birdseed, some broken up stale bread and grated apple or carrot. Mix it all together and mould it into a ball shape.

2. Feed a piece of string through the centre of the ball and place in the fridge to harden.

3. Attach the fat ball to a tree or bird hotspot and watch the birds go wild.

Give the birdies a bath

A birdbath can become a focal point in the garden –
and the birds will help by eating up those nasty bugs.

1. Choose a bath with simple, sloping sides so that
various bird species can avail themselves of its facilities.
The surface should be rough. Fill the bath with water,
2.5 cm (1 in) deep. Site near some bushes to allow the
birds to take cover if need be.

2. Keep the birdbath clean and topped up with fresh
water. Check regularly for ice in winter.

Growing with wild abandon

**An unkempt hedge can be home to all
manner of birdlife.**

1. Instead of trimming your bushes, leave them to
grow *au naturel*. This will provide a safe and secure
habitat for birds – and a threatening environment
for bad bugs.

Be nice to the bees

Bees don't eat garden enemies but they're vital for a healthy and stable garden. Choose plants that are rich in nectar to help your bees thrive.

1. Plant sweetpeas, lupins and foxgloves, honeysuckle and buddleja.

2. The plants will be pollinated, the bees will have as much pollen and nectar as they need and your garden will flourish.

Go for gold!

**Hoverflies are always welcome in the garden –
they feed on aphids and pollinate flowers in a similar
way to bees.**

1. Hoverflies need a great deal of energy to be able to
hover and go about their daily business. They need to
refuel regularly with a sweet drink of nectar and
particularly love golden yellow flowers such as
marigolds. To ensure their presence in your garden,
just say it with flowers.

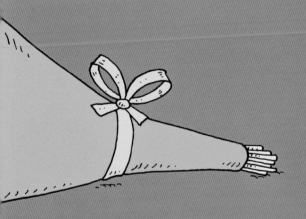

Sorted by pond life

Frogs, toads and newts love nothing more than
a slug supper.

1. You'll be amazed at the amount of wildlife a small
pond will attract to your garden.

2. Within no time you'll find a frog has made itself
at home. These predators are loved by gardeners
everywhere, as they'll eat anything they can get in
their mouths.

THE
END

Index

Acknowledgements

Executive Editor • **Sarah Ford**
Editor • **Fiona Robertson**
Design Manager • **Tokiko Morishima**
Illustrator • **KJA-artists.com**
Senior Production Controller • **Manjit Sihra**